Krystal R. Lee

SURVIVOR

Broken, But Not Discarded

Literacy
IN MOTION

Published by Literacy in Motion
555 Galaria Way Chandler AZ 85226

Anthony KaDarrell Thigpen editorial services, a subsidiary of Literacy in Motion. (Anthony_Thigpen@aol.com)

Library of Congress Cataloging-in-Publication Data Publisher and Printing by Literacy in Motion   Cover Design by Literacy in Motion Design Team

SURVIVOR
ISBN: 978-0-9904440-4-6

Graphics and Editing by Anthony KaDarrell Thigpen

Self-Help and Religious Printed in the United States of America

Dedication and Special Thanks

I am always humbled and grateful for God's grace, mercy, and unconditional love. I submit my testimony into the loving arms of my best friend and husband, Ray A. Lee, Jr., because you never gave up on me. I dedicate this book to my babies, Destinee, LaDajah, Anthony, and Ray III. Special thanks to Lacillia Jones, one of my greatest encouragers, professor Kristin Latour, my family, and my church family at House of Glory Ministries.

Krystal R. Lee

CONTENT

Chapter 1
My Testimony is Not My Biography

My name is Krystal Renee Lee, and I was born August 24, 1984. I'm the sister to four brothers, of whom one is now deceased. I'm a wife and mother of four beautiful children: Destinee, LaDajah, Anthony and Ray III. I currently serve as the First Lady of House of Glory Ministries. This is not a biography or tell-all book. This is my testimony. I'm not proud of my mistakes, but everything happens for a purpose. I pray that it serves as a tool to let readers know that despite what has gone wrong in their lives, it's possible to make it. You will survive. I pray that hearts and minds will change after reading this book and generational curses are broken. As I share with you my story, I pray that it

> **This is not a biography or tell-all book. This is my testimony.**

encourages the young as well as old to let go of the things that have caused hurt and pain to control their lives. There could be no stories without experiences, whether good or bad. Just as there are no messages without surviving life's worse mess, and no testimony without enduring unwanted test.

I don't know about you, but I've had many times in my life where I felt that I was not going to make it. I didn't feel like a survivor when I was at my lowest. **The experiences that life deals us seem so hard, but there is light at the end of the tunnel.** Some things cut and bruise your spirit so deeply that you feel all hope and strength is forever lost, but there is hope. The good thing about life is that you're allowed to make choices and decisions, and if you don't like the outcome, you have the power to change it. As long as there is breath in your body, you can make it. **We have to learn how to take the good and the**

7

bad and still find a way to smile. Keep living and keep reading and I will show you how to do just that.

I'm reminded of the Apostle Paul and how he experienced so much adversity in life because of the assignment that God gave him. He managed to survive with the strength of the Lord. The Eurocydon Storm was one of the situations that he had to face in his life. This storm was so brutal that everyone that was involved in it prepared to die, but Paul was not worried. **Stop worrying.** Paul wasn't worried because he received an assignment from God that he was determined to accomplish. I take great joy in this story because despite what happened to him, and around him, he focused on the assignment that God had given him. This storm damaged everything around him, even the ship that they were in, but because of his faith in God, everyone was spared. They were able to make it to shore on broken pieces.

You might be standing in the midst of your storm watching your life fall to pieces. Perhaps you have no idea how you're going to make it. Maybe you've already given up and thrown in the towel, but God is still in control. We were all predestined to be great, and God knew our stories far before we were formed in our mothers' wombs. We can be secure in knowing that the Lord will not put more on us than we can bear. If He brought us to it, He's faithful and will get us through it. My experiences might not be the same as everyone else's, but He's able to fix anything that has caused brokenness.

Being a part of a family where females were scarce left me vulnerable right from the start. Having no sisters and all uncles proved to be more difficult than one would think. I didn't care to play with dolls and feminine things of that nature. I had no choice but to be tough because that's all that I knew. I spent a lot of my childhood in the projects with my grandmother because my mom worked evenings. I learned how to fight and defend myself at an early age; I quickly became a product of my environment. As a child, I was in situations that no young person should have to face.

Many don't believe in generational curses, but I'm a living witness that they do exist. The enemy is not satisfied with just destroying one generation. The devil wants to destroy every generation of your family, just as God wants every generation of your family to be abundantly blessed.

> **The devil wants to destroy every generation of your family, just as God wants every generation of your family to be abundantly blessed.**

There are the curses of addictions, poverty, sexual abuse and diseases. As quiet as it is kept, every family has experienced something that seems to get handed down from generation to generation, whether sociological, biological or economical. There has to be someone spiritual enough to say, "The curse ends with me." The blood that Jesus Christ shed on the cross made it possible to cancel every attack and assignment that the enemy places over your family. Nobody wants to talk about what they face because they are

9

afraid that people will look at them differently, and they may. We should not allow the enemy to steal our testimony because we fear how others might view us. **Truth is, we overcome by the blood of the lamb and the words of our testimony. Silence is one of the ways that the enemy keeps you in bondage, but it's time to break free.**

Chapter 2
Break Free

The first step in breaking free is acknowledging that something has you bound. Oftentimes, we experience tragic events in our lives, and we learn to suppress the feelings so that we don't feel the hurt. Suppressing feelings is unhealthy. **Denial often leads to an unexpected source of depression. The reality is that if you don't handle your issue, your issue will eventually handle you. Don't be passive – handle it.**

There have been women who have gone through life bitter and angry because of any given single event. For example, I'm a witness that when your innocence is taken, you feel broken, hurt, isolated, and alone – making you skeptical of everyone. There are consequences for every action that is taken, whether you deal with the situation or not.

My first great challenge of being molested was not an easy task to handle as a child. As I write, I can remember feelings I had and the questions that would never be answered because I was too ashamed and embarrassed to say anything. I

> **Being a survivor has more to do with how you handle situations, not necessarily who caused them.**

felt psychologically silenced by my circumstances. The feeling of being alone in my secret became an everyday torment for me. **Mixed emotions and misguided thoughts are confusing, discouraging, and extremely frustrating – I needed help.** I wondered why I was going through this and why no one would help me. As a child, I felt like a super hero would one day come and save me from what was going on, but it never happened. No one rescued me. I began to get used to it and figured every little girl probably goes through this, so I dealt with it – so I thought. I merely became numb to the pain? As I began to get older, the memories never left. I would sometimes look at the ones who had caused the pain and wonder if they even remembered or felt bad about what they had done. Being a survivor has more to do with how you handle situations, not necessarily who caused them.

The enemy starts working and plotting as soon as we are born. That is why so many unusual crimes take place against infants and toddlers. The enemy hates the innocence that children possess, and aims to kill, steal and destroy their lives. For this very reason it is vitally important to be watchful and prayerful over young children. He is like a thief prowling for an open door. He is very cunning, and doesn't care whom he uses to get the job done. It doesn't hurt to warn your children of the dangers that are awaiting them and always keep an open line of communication with them. The devil counts on us being secretive because he's able to make his best move in darkness.

Unless you have been a victim of mental, sexual, or physical abuse, it'll be difficult to comprehend the intensity of hurt that goes along with it. A child is mentally and physically crushed when his or her space has been invaded and innocence suddenly snatched. The hurt and pain never leaves; as a matter of fact it grows with the child.

As I grew older, I had so many different feelings, but I learned to suppress them because I knew I would never tell a soul what I was going through. If I did, who would even believe me anyway?

There are a lot of women and men who have gone through this, but I'm here to tell you, don't give up. You will make it. There is a God who can heal every wound, and He's able to turn around everything for your good. Maybe you didn't experience molestation, physical or mental abuse, but perhaps you grew up in poverty.

Living in poverty is just as common in America as molestation. Poverty has become all too common to certain races, and the drive to do better has been lost. Poverty is a disease and curse that has plagued many races for generations. It's not God's will that any children live without their needs being met. The event or environment that surrounds you doesn't have to keep you from being great.

> **Oftentimes, we look at what others are doing and compare ourselves, but their success doesn't dictate your destiny.**

Having a mindset, "My mom and dad lived in poverty, so there is no hope for me," is not the answer. Even worse, some people don't even think about whether or not life could be better, they just accept what is.

I'm here to let everyone who reads this book know that you can make it and to not settle. God wants what's best for you. If you have the time and energy to complain, then there is time to make a change. God created each of us for special reasons. We all have something in us that someone can learn from. Remember that someone is watching you and saying, "If that person can do better, so can I."

I spiraled downward to a place in life where I was tired of never having enough. I was tired of not even having enough to make it from check to check. I knew that I wasn't created to just work a minimum wage job and be content. I began to complain inwardly and question my very reason for living. I asked God, "Why am I in this situation? Why are people who I went to school with doing better than me?" I began to critique and examine decisions that I made whether good or bad. I realized that I chose to go the route that my feet were traveling. Yes, I veered off course, but God began to show me that He could turn everything around for my good. Oftentimes, we look at what others are doing and compare ourselves, but their success doesn't dictate your destiny. We all have our own stories and have our own path that we must walk.   Many times we want someone to blame for our shortcomings, but if we are honest, we can't blame no one but ourselves. People can hinder you, but they cannot stop you from doing anything your heart desires. We may not get everything right the first or second time around, but we can grow in spite of our mistakes and try again. Nothing or no one that is great happened overnight.   Any successful person will tell you that it took many sleepless nights, tests and trials to be the person that they are today. So, when tribulation comes your way, difficulties, distress, and distractions, remember that God has a greater destiny designed for your life. This hope will give you the strength to break free. You have to see yourself the way God sees you.

Chapter 3
Push Pass Your Past

Never let past failures keep you down, depressed and in the dumps. Keep telling yourself, "I am a victor, not a victim." Keep believing in the your future. Forget those things that are behind you and press toward a greater tomorrow. As long as there is breath in your body, you can change your situation for the better. If you believe that things will get better, then things will get better. Even if you are reading this book with tears in your eyes, pain in your heart and suffering from a broken spirit; there is always hope and help, if you want it.

> **If you believe that things will get better, then things will get better. Even if you are reading this book with tears in your eyes, pain in your heart and suffering from a broken spirit; there is always hope and help, if you want it.**

The enemy knows that he can keep the cycles going in our lives if we remain ignorant of his devices. This is why you can't stay stuck on yesterday's situation, no matter how bad it hurts. The devil knows that people will protect their loved ones by sweeping certain subjects under the rug. Many families are secretly hurting because issues that need to be addressed are forbidden, and therefore no healing or forgiving can ever take place. In order to push pass your past you must first break free.

Issues left unresolved will cause a person to go through life broken – and brokenness leads to emotional bondage. Unresolved things have been known to cause illnesses physically and mentally. The enemy desires for issues to consume you insomuch that you'll wish you were dead. You can feel so dirty and unworthy to the point where you feel that God doesn't even love you. **Many men and women have taken their own lives because they didn't know how to process the pain that they were feeling. I never got to the point of contemplating suicide, but I was numb to life - nothing no longer had meaning – it was as if I had no respect for life.**

Numbness will cause you to miss the blessings God places along your journey to bring you joy. Your issues can stop you from fulfilling your purpose in life, and then hinder others. In other words, you are a part of a much larger puzzle – and you possess a piece of life that actually serves an amazing purpose. Try to remember that we are not living life just for ourselves, but everyone's destiny is a link in a greater chain.

Weighted down with pressures of dealing with the pain that's too heavy for you to carry will drain the very life out of you. When you allow your issues to strip you, it causes you to lose your love for others and become bitter. The moment this happens, your guards are put up, and nobody is let in, and the pain isn't let out. Pain will cause you to isolate yourself from others if left unresolved – and isolation is imprisonment.

Isolation is one of the greatest weapons that the enemy uses to destroy men and women all over the world. Many are deceived into believing that they can deal with a problem on their own, but that is not true. As a child, I remember singing in the district choir, and we sang a song with the lyrics: **"No man is an island, you can't make it alone, you need me and I need you to carry on."** As a child, I couldn't comprehend the magnitude of the message, but I truly understand it now. You can't be so caught up in being perfect and how everyone will view you. Worrying that others will find you, or discover your secrets, will eat you alive. Being prideful is self-inflicted pain. How will we overcome these issues if everyone is scared to talk about them?

I'm reminded of the woman in Luke with the issue of blood. The continuous flow of blood made her unclean, and she was looked upon as a diseased woman. Nobody wanted to be seen with her, and she wasn't even allowed to enter into the temple to worship because of this issue. This woman spent all she had and went to every physician, and they still had no remedy for the situation. Could you conceive the pain and loneliness that this woman felt? She finally got to the point that

> **I had to face the fact that my self-diagnosis and antidotes of denial did not remedy my pain. I needed help.**

she broke the rules and went out among the people after hearing that Jesus was passing by. This woman didn't let what could have happened or the way people looked at her detour her heart. She was determined to be healed at any cost.

If this woman had drowned in self-pity and just grasped on to the idea that there was no hope, she would have let her issue win, but she didn't. She had come to the realization that she needed help. I had to face the fact that my self-diagnosis and antidotes of denial did not remedy my pain. I needed help. We have to realize that our issues are making us sick, and we can't cure it on our own no matter how hard we try.

Often we try to go through life with our issues and act as if they don't exist. I don't agree with the statement that time heals all wounds; that's a long stretch from the truth. Time allows you to learn how to cope with things, but the experience remains etched into your soul. I found myself in a situation where I was having a discussion with someone whom I loved. He hadn't agreed with a statement that I had made and demanded that I give him an apology. We went back and forth for a while until I blurted out, "If I owe you an apology, then you owe me one for all the bad things that happened to me in my childhood." Now grown, a first lady, a wife and mother, yet my childhood poked its head into my passionate conversation. I thought that I had left this issue on the altar, but I realized on that day I had not.

There have been so many wounded people who have tried to heal themselves by getting into new relationships. That strategy is proven to fail.

Life lessons did not teach me that time nor relationships can heal unresolved emotional wounds. See, I had been broken as a child, but the Lord didn't allow for it to destroy me. I was damaged but not discarded, and the Lord knew that someone would need to hear how I overcame.

There have been so many wounded people who have tried to heal themselves by getting into new relationships. That strategy is proven to fail. The only way that you will receive true healing is by giving your pain to Jesus. There is no relationship that can take away what someone else did to hurt you. Seasonal happiness might pacify your pain temporarily, but the pain will surface. It only takes one bad argument or a difficult discussion to reopen a wound that you once thought was healed. One of the reasons why people are walking around hurting is because forgiveness has not taken place.

Chapter 4
Forgiveness

Forgiveness is much harder than a lot of people think, but it is necessary. When you experience being deeply hurt, you want others to feel what you're experiencing. We have to learn how to forgive even if the person who hurt us never apologizes. Forgiveness benefits the person offering it because *unforgiveness* and bitterness have been known to cause sickness.

Forgiveness is liberating. It also prevents the enemy from occupying space in your heart. He seeks to devour you in any way that he can. If we refuse to forgive and hold on to our pain, our Father in heaven will not forgive us, and the enemy knows just that. I challenge each and every reader to search your heart and let go of grudges and bitterness. The

> **We have to learn how to forgive even if the person who hurt us never apologizes.**

Lord will help you forgive those who have caused you pain. Repent for holding *unforgiveness* in your heart. Break the chains of bitterness and hatred. Break free from these emotions that seek to keep you down and distressed. It is your decision to determine what you allow to remain in your heart. We can't control everything that happens in our life. When the people who should or could have protected you fail, you have to forgive them as well. Parents are not super heroes and have things going in their lives, but it's their job to pay attention and be there for children when things do happen. Parents can't be with their children 24 hours a day, but you should know your child enough to realize something has changed in their lives. Parents need to be watchful, because the enemy only needs a little space to invade. Yes, children go through phases while growing up, but some actions are a cry out for help.

As I began to reflect on my childhood, my mind zoomed in on a problem that I had. I struggled with stealing, and yes, I know you are saying every child has stolen, but this situation was different. My parents did very well financially, and my brothers and I pretty much got everything that we asked for, so I couldn't answer why I had this problem. I knew that this behavior was unacceptable and that it would cause me to receive a whooping. I was in grade school when I remember this problem started to manifest. I would steal my teacher's gum, and it wasn't even the kind of gum a child my age would like. I don't know why I kept doing it, but I would see her go for her gum and look puzzled when she was unable to find it. I guess she got fed up and decided to set up a trap to catch who was taking her gum. Somehow she had marked her gum sticks, and I was caught with the wrappers, and you can guess what happened. Anytime you can keep doing wrong, and you know the consequences and still can't stop, there is a problem. Some people don't believe that spirits can control children, but I do. There are a few stories in the Bible where children were possessed or under the control of spirits, one being the little girl who could tell people their future. When you know something is wrong, and you can't control yourself, you're under the direction of an ungodly spirit.

The Lord is so gracious that He allows us to be exposed. Exposure is good because a lot of people wouldn't admit they have a problem. Spirits attach themselves to children in many ways. Nowadays our children are able to play violent games, watch violent and nasty films, and also listen to explicit music. We open our children up to the enemy because these things keep them quiet, but this is another trick of the enemy.

As a parent, you may not be in the place you should be in with God, but it's a must that the Word of God begins to be instilled in your child at a young age. Take your children to Sunday school so they can be taught. The Word says to train up a child in the way that they should go and when they're older, they won't depart from it. Our world today is running crazy because of the lack of training. It was in Sunday school that I learned how to love others despite their race; it was in Sunday school where I learned that Jesus wouldn't be happy if I lied and stole. It was the teachers and Sunday school books that explained how and why to ask for forgiveness if I went against His Word. If more parents took the time out to teach and bring or send their children to church, there would not be so much hatred, evil, and unforgiveness in the world. The enemy starts working on children at a young age because of the call that's on their lives. I'm thankful for every adult who took the time to pour the Lord's message into me as a child because as an adult, it has helped me. I had a gift of singing, and it was because of the young adults that sang at church that I became interested in using it.

As I began to mature and become active in church, I figured out the "DOs and DON'Ts." My heart desired to be used by the Lord, but at the same time I was full of issues. It's impossible to be souled out for God and be bounded by the demons of your past, but I hadn't quite learned how to release them.

What I really was doing was hiding behind a mask every time I entered the sanctuary. I was learning how to be deceitful and putting up a front to the people at church. I wasn't the sweet Krystal who many thought I was. I was broken, and I had no idea how to pick up the

> **I had no idea how powerful forgiveness was, even though God had sent His Son to suffer and sacrifice in effort to forgive me.**

pieces and put them back together. I had no idea how powerful forgiveness was, even though God had sent His Son to suffer and sacrifice in effort to forgive me. I was gifted with a strong soprano voice, I focused on that, and oftentimes missed the message.

Many have gifts and talents, and they hide behind them because they have nothing else to hang on to. My gift of singing gave me the desired attention I craved, and it coated the hurt that was lying dormant. As I aged, I began to feel like two people were living in my body.

> **It was very exhausting trying to be something that I was not.**

It was very exhausting trying to be something that I was not. At the age of sixteen, I found out that I was pregnant, and I was just a junior in high school, working a part time job. What in the world was I going to do with a baby? I was in a relationship, but I really didn't know what love was. Our relationship was unstable because the things that I went through in my childhood caused a lot of issues between us. I didn't know how to handle disagreements without being hostile because I was used to having things go my way. I would become outraged and violent toward him, and he was not that type of man. I would act out so badly sometimes, I would feel horrible because there wasn't a logically reason for what I had done. Later I learned that the only way to let go of my issues was to forgive the parties that caused them. It's not easy forgiving someone who doesn't care about how his or her actions damaged your life.

Chapter 5
Building on a Broken Foundation

My boyfriend continued to stick by my side throughout the pregnancy even though he seldom had the energy to deal with me. So there I was pregnant, full of unwanted issues, and hormone changes that seemingly intensified the rage that was already in me. I can recall one incident that happened while my brother and I were walking home. I don't remember how the conversation started, but I remember my brother calling me stupid and saying I was dumb for getting pregnant while I was still in school. I reacted violently to what he was saying and scratched his face up really badly. I didn't know what got into me, and I couldn't believe I had done that. It was also a lesson for me. I became even more determined to make it through school because people were expecting me to fail. I was so heartbroken by the things he said, but I never told anybody, so yet again I found myself dealing with hurt on my own. No matter how sick or tired I felt, I pressed my way to school and managed to excel with honors through my entire pregnancy.

July 11, 2001, Destinee Camaree Lee, came on the scene and changed my life forever. I was now a mother, and I had to bury my hurt and pain deep beneath my subconscious. Caring for Destinee's future seemed far greater than wrestling with the spirits of my painful past. At six weeks old, she attended my high school daycare. I thank God every time I think about the ladies who were so understanding and kind to every teenage mom who walked into that door. We became family and a few of them even came to our wedding soon after. These women, even though it was their job, were like angels to us, and we felt comfortable leaving our babies in their hands.

Safety was a big issue with me, and I had already made up in my mind that my child would not go through what I experienced.

New relationships do not heal, change or cancel the fact that you are a mess and full of issues. I wanted to tell my husband so badly what I was going through emotionally, but it wasn't an easy thing to do. I felt that if I would tell him what my life had been like before he came into the picture, he wouldn't want me anymore. I feared that if I would release these problems to him, he would look at me differently as if I was dirty, so rather then tell him, I continued to be hostile towards him – and feel dirty at the same time.

I'm so thankful that he decided to stick by my side despite my actions towards him. I believe that God sent him to prevent me from self-destructing. What we fail to realize is that God is almighty and a great deliverer, but He

> God knows our ending, even when we're stuck at the beginning.

uses people to draw you closer to Him when you're too blind. At the time we were going through our problems, as my boyfriend, he didn't understand why he couldn't just walk away and be with someone else, but God's ways are not our ways. God knows our ending, even when we're stuck at the beginning.

We continued on with our relationship, and the problems still existed, but there was a bond between us that couldn't be broken. No matter who felt we should let the relationship go, we decided to stick it out. There are some things that we are meant to have. Time went on, and we continued with the same problems, but we loved each other, so we decided that we would get married after I graduated. A few months before graduation, I felt that I may have been pregnant, but I ignored the signs and continued on about my business. After graduation, we were going to have his dad marry us without having a formal ceremony, until my godmother intervened. She told me that I should have a wedding because I was the only daughter that my parents had and that it would rob my dad of giving his only daughter away. We decided to prepare a wedding ceremony with only a few months to stay on schedule for our September date.

I began to plan the wedding and look for my wedding dress. A few weeks after that I began to experience other symptoms that could not be ignored, so I decided to take a pregnancy test. The results were in; I was pregnant, to my surprise. I was devastated; everything that I had hoped and planned for now seemed to be going down the drain. The dream that I had to go away for college was not even an option now. I was going to be a mother for the second time, and I was only 18 years old. I went through a mild depression and cried and threw temper tantrums, but all that was in vain because the doctor said she would be here in five months. I did not want to enter into a marriage like this; I didn't want another baby.

I got over it. I finally came to grips with the fact that she was coming, and there was nothing I could do about it. We went ahead with the wedding plans, and I moved out of my parent's house to start a blissful life of marriage. I finally entered into a union that was created and honored by God. I finally felt like I was doing something right. We moved in with a lady from the church saying she'd help us get on our feet. I was five months pregnant, with a one year old and a husband sleeping in a basement sharing a twin size bed. I said, "Lord there has got to be something better than this." This living arrangement didn't last long because after a few weeks this woman, who said she would help us, gave us a formal letter raising the rent.

That day I told my husband, "I can't do this anymore." I was uncomfortable and didn't want to stay there any longer. He decided to ask his mother if we could stay with them, and his parents welcomed us. Everything was going fine; we would have our little disagreements here and there but nothing worth mentioning – barely memorable.

I was getting used to being a wife even though some things that he expected was unusual for me. I don't recall the details, but I do remember us having a huge argument - it was a big one. It's one thing to fight behind closed doors, but it's another thing when others know about it. We had so many things working against us, but we kept fighting for our marriage. We continued learning from one another and planning the future of our family. No matter how much we planned, it seemed like things would not come together. We were trying to better ourselves with jobs, but it was difficult because we were sharing a vehicle. Not having enough started to take a toll on me, not to mention all my other baggage.

One day after dropping my husband off, I felt that my water bag might have broken. This was serious; I was only six months along, and this was not supposed to be happening. I brushed it off until I felt to need to rush to the hospital. Once I was there and checked in, I found out that my bag had ruptured and that the baby would be here soon. There was a big chance that my expected child would not be able to survive. There I was, alone, everyone I loved was at work. The child that I threw a fit about having was not expected to make it. I will never forget the nurse who came into the room and told me that if my child even survived, she would only have a few fingers and be mentally retarded. The way she said it was so cold and done without love that it caused me to just lie in the bed and cry. I began to think of all the complaining and my mean-spirited when I initially found out that I was pregnant, and I began to repent. We have to be aware that death and life are in the power of our own tongue, and we can curse our own lives. I was transported to Rush Hospital in Chicago, and my mom started calling people to pray for me. After running all kinds of painful tests, the doctors at Rush determined that my bag was no longer leaking, and they released me. From that day, I learned the true power of prayer, and I was able to carry her to term. Ladajah Rae Lee was born December 27, 2002 – she was healthy and whole. My God performed a miracle on my behalf and blessed us with another healthy, beautiful baby girl. Watching her grow up and seeing her gifts allowed me to see why she is here. I realize why the enemy tried to stop her from entering the world. Whenever the devil fights you even before you're born, God has something great in store for you. My husband and I began to adapt to having two children.

The Lord opened a door for us. My husband started a full time job, and things began to look up. We got our own home, and it finally felt like things were coming together. During this time, I also started working a better job and got another vehicle. When things should have been looking up, the problems got worse; I found myself pregnant again and miserable. The job I worked pulled me out of church three Sundays a month, and that definitely was no good. **I began to whither spiritually, and our marriage problems increased. I was depressed, living in denial, and we just couldn't seem to get things right.** I would get mad and move out and come back and continued on this merry-go-round for years. I had so much anger and resentment in my heart and didn't know how to release it. I turned to people who I shouldn't have and made our problems worse. I began to confide in a man, and that was my biggest mistake. The enemy will use every crack that he can to get into your life. I began to develop feelings for this man because he was always there to listen to me when I needed it. So not only was I dealing with my marriage issues, I had now brought more complication into my already confused world. The fact that I knew I could lean on him made it easier to walk away from my husband when I got mad and didn't agree with something. I left my husband, moved in with my parents, and continued my unhealthy friendship. My life was becoming more and more complicated, but it was only about to get worse.

I had my third child January 8, 2007, and I went to my parents' house afterward. I stayed there for a few weeks and then went back to my husband. Things were going good for a while, but soon after I left again. Here I was moving three children back home with my parents.

I started talking to all the wrong people, thinking I had all the right reasons. I developed relationships that felt meaningful, but violated my marriage. I was separated, but married, entertaining the wrong company, and looking for happiness in all the wrong places. I how did I get here? What kind of young mother was I becoming? I was confusing temporary happiness with love. I still loved my husband, but my actions didn't align with my heart.

Despite my brokenness, I joined a community choir. The choir allowed me to keep my mind off of all the drama that was going on in my life. **Hurt people find others things to do to keep their minds distracted from what matters.** I continued in this crazy triangle of mismanaged relationships, irresponsibility, and confusion until I just couldn't handle any more.

I walked away from a messy Saturday night situation straight into the doors of the church. After the message, I went up for prayer. I knew my life was not going down the right path. I don't remember everything that the women of God prayed, but I do remember her saying, "It can work, but you have to change and be submissive." Finally I had gotten my answer. It was not for me to get a divorce. I could have easily gotten remarried, but that wasn't God's plan for my life. The change had to be made within me, and I was determined to do it. I wanted my husband and my family together again.

I remember talking to God and asking Him to help me. I started by asking forgiveness. I cried out for Him to reconnect me with my husband. This was a big shocker to my family and friends after all, we had both seemed to have moved on with our lives. I had even filed for a divorce, and the courts agreed to pay for it. I had moved out of my parents' house, and my husband had just got hired at a new job, and I agreed to let him use my address. God works in mysterious ways.

Chapter 6
New Beginnings

Using my address at his new job, somehow led to my husband moving in, and we began to work on our marriage. I was still in a state of shock because I couldn't believe that the Lord had allowed us to reconnect after all that had taken place. After maybe about a month or two, the courts mailed the preliminary divorce papers. He asked me what did I want to do. The Lord had blocked our divorce, and all I could do was smile. I had made up in my mind that I was tired of my life being on a merry-go-round, and that I was happy about the direction God was taking my life in. We began to talk to one another about things that each of us felt was wrong, and truly, we had learned from our mistakes. I also felt horrible that other hearts were broken in the process, but there was nothing that I could do but say that I was sorry. I will never forget my mother-in-law saying, "Before you open another door, make sure the other door is shut." I could never take back the pain that I caused others, but I was truly sorry.

I will never forget my mother-in-law saying, "Before you open another door, make sure the other door is shut."

My life was finally on track, and we were beginning to start back going to church together because I had also started a job that was Monday through Friday. Things were looking up, and I had the Lord to thank. Things were going so well that we planned to have another baby.

A couple of weeks before Christmas, I found out I was pregnant, and I was going to put the test under the Christmas tree, but I was so excited I couldn't wait. January 8, 2004 we welcomed our final child, Ray

Anthony Lee III, into the world. The Lord had revived our family, and I was glad.

The only way that you will break the curses off your life is to come to grips with the fact that there is a problem, and you need to fix it before you miss out on what God has in store for you. Our marriage was doing well and things were going great. The Lord began to refresh and renew me in my mind as well as in my heart. Things began to line up in our spiritual lives as well.

It was the year of new beginnings for our marriage, and also the year where my husband would answer the call to become a pastor. I was so fearful of what people would say because of our past and also because we were so young. I didn't know how it was going to happen because of our finances, and also because we were active in the church that we were attending. I knew that this

> **I knew that this wasn't going to be an easy task, but I realized that we didn't have a choice in the matter because God mandated it.**

wasn't going to be an easy task, but I realized that we didn't have a choice in the matter because God mandated it.

Whenever God gives you something to do, you have to be ready for a battle because the enemy fights anything that God ordains. My husband wrestled to make the decision but finally gave in and started planning for the opening of the House of Glory Church.

We heard so much negativity from people that we frequented churches with. One pastor even told my husband that she foresaw death if he went on with the plans for the new church, and she talked about me so badly that she couldn't even look at me. As my husband began to tell me the things that she had shared, it seemed as if the devil was speaking right through her. It bothered us so badly that both of us took off work the next day. We have to be mindful that the enemy will do anything and use anybody to detour us from what the Lord has called for us to do. **Interesting how naysayers watched silently on the sidelines when our marriage was deteriorating, but once God reunited us and started our journey in the ministry we hear unwanted voices.** You can't be moved to the point that you let people destroy the call on your life. People will become jealous and put limitations on your assignments because they don't understand or they simply just don't want you to succeed. There are no depths that the enemy won't go to keep you from fulfilling your purpose.

I found out that people who kiss and even encourage you sometimes stab you in the back. When you say yes to the call of Jesus, it gets the attention of the devil. Watch what you allow people to speak over your life. Know the difference between people who prey and believers who pray. People will try to put a time limit on what God has told you to do. They will attempt to spew doubt in your spirit about if it was God that spoke to you.

> **Know the difference between people who prey and believers who pray.**

Doubt will destroy the movement of God. It is impossible to please God without faith, and that is the biggest thing that the enemy attacks. Be secure in your relationship with God, insomuch that you're able to know without a shadow of a doubt what the Lord who spoke to you. You must move forward in Christ, and everything else will line up. Your "yes" to God will show you who is really for you or against you. People will love you and pat you on the back when you're doing things that they agree with. We found this out very early in our new walk that we are on.

I never knew the hurt and pain that people and their tongues could do. Growing up I often quoted "sticks and stones may beak my bones but words will never hurt me." I found out just how wrong I was – words can hurt. The people that we helped out of loyalty, were not there when we needed them the most. I had been so consumed with what others were doing that I had pushed the assignment of to the side. The Lord had to remind me that it was not about the naysayers.

I remembered what a church mother told me about prayer at this time. She told me, "Child if you've never prayed before, you will once you become a first lady," my God, she was right. Even though I prayed previously, I didn't have a real prayer life. I was pushed into the woman and prayer intercessor I am today.

God used people to speak over my life, even when it was in an uproar, now I am doing exactly what they spoke. I never thought I would be the person in the forefront leading praise and worship and prayer. Who would have ever thought that broken little girl would become a First Lady in October 2010, at age 26? I look back on my childhood and think, this is why I wasn't destroyed because I had a greater destiny. Even though I went through some of the worse experiences imaginable during my childhood, my testimony is designed to help someone else survive. We need to realize that we don't go through pain just to go through it, but to help bring someone else out.

Chapter 7
The Silhouette of a Survivor

There are levels to growth and anointing, and you don't know what someone has to go through because of the call on their life. Yes, I experienced deep hurt as a child, but I had no idea that I could experience anything worse than that until I received a phone call August 16, 2012.

I remember visiting Posen, IL to hear Bishop Blake preach at Abounding Life Church. My phone rang repeatedly. I heard my mom crying on the voicemail, and my dad saying, "Return the call. It's an emergency." I called my mom, and all I can remember is my mom saying, "They shot him up!" I immediately screamed and started shaking. I was in disbelief. We left the church and headed to the Silver Cross hospital.

That was the longest ride I had ever been on. I couldn't believe it. My mind was all over the place. Just a few days before, I had seen a statement that my brother had written on Facebook, and I had told him that whatever was going on, it was not that serious. He informed me that he was okay, but it just didn't set well in my spirit. I got off Facebook and said a little prayer to the Lord: I don't know what is going on with him but please protect him.

My brother had been shot multiple times. After waiting, we were informed that his condition was poor and that he was probably not going to make it through the night. The doctor was so cold as if my brother was just another black thug that nobody cared about, but he wasn't. He was a college graduate and a father to two, and on that night we found out he would be a dad again. The doctor's words sent me straight to me knees. God had been trying to warn me for some time, but I had brushed it off.

Kyle was transported to Oak Lawn hospital, and we raced up there to see him. When we arrived, an officer greeted us, and I felt horrible in my spirit, but I still had an ounce of help in me. We were getting on the elevator, and a man stopped the elevator. I saw the title "Chaplain" on his badge, and I just felt like a part of my existence was dying, but I remained quiet. They escorted us to what they call the Quiet Room. I wanted to know the location and condition of my brother. The doctor came in, and I wasn't prepared for the words that were about to come out of her mouth. She started off by saying, "You guys know what Kyle was going through, and I'm sorry, he didn't make it." I flipped out. I cried. I jumped. Oh Lord, this can't be happening. I began to tell myself it wasn't true. I created an explanation to eliminate the pain: He had to play dead because maybe he was in the Special Forces like the men in the movies. One of his dreams was to become a police officer. The hurt and pain that I felt was unbearable. All I could say is, "my brother is gone. He's gone." The hurt was so unbearable that I didn't even have the energy to hate the person that had caused this. This pain can never be described until you actually go through it, but I pray that nobody ever experiences this magnitude of pain. As if things couldn't get any worse, his burial preparations to place on my birthday. I felt like I was being punished for something I had done. I went through the traditional stages of grief.

First, I blamed myself, as I began to come to the conclusion that his death was real. I felt that if I would have prayed more seriously then my brother would still be alive. I had to realize that just because we pray doesn't mean that every bad thing will stop. The day after my brother's funeral, I went to church, and the pastor talked about Job and how he was a righteous man, but the enemy was still allowed to destroy his property and kill his children.

Anytime you trust in God and live life the way the Bible says, you become the center of attention. I'm a firm believer that everything will work out for the good for those who love the Lord. I knew I loved Him, but I didn't understand how anything good would stem from this. In fact things got worse when I looked at things with my natural eyes. People often say death will bring families closer or push them farther apart.

It seemed that nobody knew how to deal with my brother's death, and everybody handled it his or her own way. My brothers couldn't understand how God could let someone do this to a young man who wasn't living the street life. People often hate and question God when bad things happen and forget that we have an enemy that is also on assignment. We all know that the devil aims to kill,

I realized that God created a survivor inside of me.

steal and destroy. He doesn't care how good you are, or your life plans, he merely knows his time is short. No man knows the day nor the hour that the Lord will appear, but we have to live each day like it's our last. It's time to get our houses in order. The Lord is on his way back. What the devil meant for evil, the Lord will turn around for your good.

We have to trust in God that no matter what we lose in this life, we still hold on to our relationship with Him. We don't have the authority to question God's sovereignty. Through the experience of my brother's death, I found out that I had things in me that I had no idea existed.

I never lost trust in God, and I couldn't believe the inner strength that I possessed. I realized that God created a survivor inside of me. Yes, I cried, cried and cried, and that is normal. There is a time to laugh and a time to mourn; everyone goes through different seasons in their lives, but we must hold on to our Faith. Looking at one of my baby brothers in a casket made me realize even more that life isn't a joke, and that death comes for the old as well as the young. His death made me appreciate my days upon the earth, and I plan to use them wisely. We focus so much on making sure we're beautiful or handsome on the outside, but we don't make sure our hearts are pure. Men look on the outside, but God is going to judge our hearts.

The little dash in between the year of your birth and death represents your life. We think we have so much time to do what we want that we neglect to ask God, "what is my purpose on this Earth?" We all were created to do something for the building of God's kingdom, but the Lord will not force His will upon anyone. As mighty as He is, He still allows us to make decisions. If the Lord can't use you for His Glory,

> **When you hold on to the hurt that others have caused, those people are holding you hostage, and going on with their own lives.**

then He has no reason to keep you alive. We are not here just to be here, but we are here to serve God and help others get to know Him. I have become a different person since losing my brother.

I'm no longer fearful of walking away from people who aren't good for me. It also made me realize that if I can forgive the person who took my brother's life, then these other grudges that I was caring weren't that serious. Carrying grudges will keep you out of the presence of God and also keep you from making it into Heaven.

When you hold on to the hurt that others have caused, those people are holding you hostage, and going on with their own lives. Don't allow others to keep you bound in your heart and keep you blinded from having a bright future. Even when people were crucifying Jesus, He asked His Father to forgive them. Jesus is our greatest example, and we should strive to be more like Him every day. There is no offense that we should not be able to forgive and move past. Forgiveness does not mean that you have to have a relationship with the people who hurt you, but it means that you love them and no longer have issues with them. It would be sad to stand before the Lord and he says, "Depart from me," because you did not forgive, and therefore, you were never forgiven for the trespasses that you had done. Examine your hurt today and let go of any issues that are keeping you from forgiving others. Ask the Lord to cleanse you and to free you from the things that shouldn't be in your spirit. I'm a witness to this form of bondage.

I held things against people, and they didn't even know, so guess who was hurt. It really only affected me. Don't let your emotions control you, instead, be in control of them. You don't have to stay defeated; there is help for you. **I challenge every person who has been broken to the point of no return, to give your issues to God. He will turn your dark days into the silhouette of a survivor.** Don't let the enemy keep you wrapped into what someone did to you, but use what happened as a stepping stone to greater things. You might not ever preach a message or write a book, but know that someone is depending on you to make it through your issue. Prove the naysayers wrong; show them that wholeness can come from brokenness.

Everything broken doesn't need to be discarded. The Lord is the glue that can put your life back together again. He was able to restore me back into His presence, and He will, and can, do the same for you.

Let the rage and bitterness that you're feeling go and replace it with words to help others be conquerors – you are survivor. I never would have imagined telling people that I was touched as a child or was an adulterous adult, but it happened and God brought me through it. I will never be ashamed to share my story because I wasn't the first one who went through hard times, and sadly, I will not be the last. There is nothing that can happen on this Earth that God didn't allow to happen. The process didn't feel good, but it worked out for my good, and I'm still alive to share some of my life's most difficult lessons – I survived.

I want you to pray this prayer with me today:

> *"Lord, You know the hands that will turn these pages, and you know them by name. You know every hurt and wound endured while walking in this life. Father, I ask*

you to touch their hearts, give them the strength to survive what others have done to them. Lord, free them today, so that they may walk in victory and be the men and women that you have called them to be. Give them the testimony that, yes, I was broken, but I didn't let it destroy me. Lord, I rejoice, because I know that you're able to deliver, and I believe that it's turning around for the good. Lord, I thank You for the opportunity to slay the demons that have been holding me back. Today, the enemy has lost another soul. Lord, forgive me for not forgiving, and thank you for reminding me that you commanded us to do so. Create in me a clean heart. I thank you for this new start. Help us all to walk in freedom and victory and seek Your face until You return, In the name of Jesus. Amen."

I pray that my assignment has been given with clarity and effectiveness. I believe that this is the season for my testimony to be released. I pray that I have exposed the enemy on every hand and that someone will become free in life because I followed the lead of the Lord. I believe that even though the Lord doesn't force Himself on anyone, He extends every tool to His people to give them the breakthrough that they need. I'm humbled that the Lord chose me at this time to be a mouthpiece to His people, and I pray that everyone who reads this book will get the healing that they need and learn the strategies of a survivor.